YOU CHOOSE

CAN YOU SURVIVE
the 1918 FLU PANDEMIC?

AN INTERACTIVE HISTORY ADVENTURE

T0008821

by Matthew K. Manning

CAPSTONE PRESS
a capstone imprint

Published by Capstone Press, an imprint of Capstone.
1710 Roe Crest Drive
North Mankato, Minnesota 56003
capstonepub.com

Library of Congress Cataloging-in-Publication Data is available
Names: Manning, Matthew K., author.
Title: Can you survive the 1918 flu pandemic? : an interactive history adventure /
  by Matthew K. Manning.
Description: North Mankato, Minnesota : Capstone Press, [2023] | Series:
  You choose: disasters in history | Includes bibliographical references. |
  Audience: Ages 8-12 | Audience: Grades 4-6
Summary: "The year is 1918. World War I is nearing its end. But the world is just
  beginning to suffer from a deadly pandemic. Within months, the deadly flu virus
  has spread around the world, infecting and killing tens of millions of people. As
  you return from the war, will you go to see your family and friends or quarantine
  to keep your loved ones safe? Will you shut down your small store to avoid
  spreading the virus? Will you quit your job as a teacher in order to stay safe,
  or continue going to school? With dozens of possible choices, it's up to YOU to
  choose how to survive through one of the worst pandemics in history"— Provided
  by publisher.
Identifiers: LCCN 2022029280 (print) | LCCN 2022029281 (ebook) |
  ISBN 9781666390834 (hardcover) | ISBN 9781666390827 (paperback) |
  ISBN 9781666390988 (pdf)
Subjects: LCSH: Influenza Epidemic, 1918-1919—Juvenile literature. |
  Influenza— History—20th century—Juvenile literature.
Classification: LCC RC150.4 .M36 2023 (print) | LCC RC150.4 (ebook) |
  DDC 614.5/1809041—dc23/eng/20220706
LC record available at https://lccn.loc.gov/2022029280
LC ebook record available at https://lccn.loc.gov/2022029281

Editorial Credits
Editor: Aaron Sautter; Designer: Bobbie Nuytten; Media Researcher: Donna
Metcalf; Production Specialist: Whitney Schaefer

TABLE OF CONTENTS

ABOUT YOUR ADVENTURE

YOU are in the middle of the worst pandemic in the modern world. The influenza outbreak of 1918 threatens every person on the planet. Soldiers fighting in World War I have helped spread the disease. Soon everyone you know will be touched by it in some way. With the virus quickly traveling across the world, YOU must decide how to avoid it. Will you and your family make it through the pandemic alive?

Chapter One sets the scene. Then you choose which path to read. Follow the directions at the bottom of the page as you read the stories. The decisions you make determine what happens next. After you finish one path, go back and read the others for new perspectives and more adventures.

Turn the page to begin your adventure.

In March 1918, several hundred soldiers suddenly became sick with the flu at Fort Riley, Kansas.

CHAPTER 1
DEADLIER THAN WAR

It is 1918 and the world is at war. They call it the Great War, but in time it will be referred to as World War I.

While the war has raged for four years, the fighting still feels new to the United States. U.S. soldiers didn't enter the conflict until 1917.

U.S. troops are now training at military bases. But they'll soon be facing an enemy unlike any they'll face in Europe. At Fort Riley in Kansas, the deadly influenza virus is spreading.

No one is sure how the outbreak began. Scientists do know that influenza, or the flu, got its start in birds. While ducks and geese aren't affected by the virus, it can be deadly for humans.

Turn the page.

Normally, the flu can't be passed directly from birds to humans. But in 1918, it's thought that an infected duck or goose flew over a pig farm and left its droppings in pig feed. The virus infected the pigs, mutated, and then passed on to a human.

Now, soldiers aren't just getting sick in Kansas. They're being shipped out to France to fight in the war. What could have been a contained epidemic is now becoming a global pandemic.

As the disease spreads around the globe, there's no vaccine to stop it. Doctors at the time understand little about how the flu is passed from one person to another. The general public knows even less.

By May, the virus reaches Spain. Nearly eight million people in that country suffer from the flu's effects. Although the disease likely started in the United States, Americans soon begin to incorrectly call the virus the "Spanish Flu."

How are you going to manage in a world filled with disease? Will you be able to avoid getting sick? Your every choice might be the difference between surviving and adding to the flu's growing death toll.

To be a U.S. soldier returning from France, turn to page 11.

To be a shop owner in Asheville, North Carolina, turn to page 43.

To be a schoolteacher in New York City, turn to page 73.

When Germany surrendered in November 1918, people celebrated the end of World War I in New York City's Times Square.

CHAPTER 2
HOME FROM THE WAR

When you enter the apartment, you notice the smell first. There's a rose scent in the air that you'd forgotten about. Your mom must have put out her special soap in the bathroom. She only uses it when a guest is coming to visit. You haven't been back home in Boston for months. You must seem like a guest to your own family.

Then you notice the framed newspaper on the wall. The headline reads "Red Sox Are The Champions." The Sox won the World Series. You can't believe you missed it. At least you saw them in the 1916 World Series. You're not too worried. You're sure they'll win again soon. It's November of 1918 now, but you're already looking forward to spring and baseball season.

Turn the page.

"You're home!" your mother yells, running toward you from the hallway. "I can't believe it!"

"Hey, ma," you say. She gives you a huge hug before you can say anything else. You've never seen her move so fast in your life.

"Oh, I'm just so glad you're safe!" she says. "And that awful war is over."

"Me, too," you say.

You've only been back in the United States for a few days. It doesn't seem real. You feel like you could wake up tomorrow and be back in France. You spent so much time in the trenches, it feels strange to be home now.

"I'm sure you've got a lot of stories, but why don't you freshen up first?" your mother suggests. "Your father will be home soon, and I've got a special meal planned."

"I kinda made plans already," you say.

"Plans? How could you have plans?" asks your mother. "You're fresh off the boat!"

"I was going to take Mandi out to dinner," you say. "I haven't seen her yet, and I wanted it to be a surprise."

"She's not family," says your mother, as she turns to head to the kitchen. "Tonight, you eat with us. You can see your girlfriend tomorrow."

"Fiancée," you correct her, as you follow her to the kitchen.

"Even your sister is coming over," your mother continues. "Her husband has been sick with that bug that's going around, so he's staying home."

She pauses and smiles at you, giving you a wink. "Not that you'll hear me complaining," she adds. "Now go to your room and relax. I'm cooking your favorite, the meatloaf with the little carrots."

Turn the page.

You smile. You know she means well, and she makes the best meatloaf. You walk down the hall and open the door to your bedroom. The bed is made with fresh sheets. Everything's much cleaner than when you left last year.

You sit down on your bed and pull out your wallet. In it is your worn black and white photo of Mandi. A night on the town seems like a great homecoming. After all, you've been fighting the Great War. You should be able to spend your first night back in Boston how you want. Yet, you really hate to disappoint your mother.

To stay home with your family, go to page 15.

To go out and celebrate with Mandi, turn to page 19.

Your mother does two things really well: cook meatloaf and give guilt trips. You know she'd be very disappointed if you left. So, you decide to stay home for family dinner.

"Look at you!" says your father, when he comes home. He gives you a big hug and almost knocks you down in the process. "Caroline, look who's home!" he adds.

Behind your father is your sister, Caroline. She looks paler than you remember. Her nose is almost bright red. She's bundled up in a huge coat. You're surprised. It's November, but it's actually a fairly warm evening. She hugs you before you can say anything.

"Are you okay?" you ask when she pulls away.

"I'm fine," she says, before suddenly sneezing right in your face.

Turn the page.

You take a step back and wipe your face with your sleeve.

"Okay, I might be a little sick," she says.

"She'll be fine," says your mother as she walks into the hall. "It's just that flu. The health commissioner himself says the worst is over. What's his name . . . Woodward? It's no big deal."

"But it *is* a big deal, ma," you say as you all head into the living room. "You wouldn't believe how many soldiers got sick from it."

You turn to Caroline. "It's serious, sis," you say. "You should be home in bed right now."

"Monty's got it too. Other than a fever and a stuffy head, he's fine," says Caroline.

"They're right," says your father. "It was bad for a bit, but they opened everything back up almost a month ago."

You remember the first time you saw the effects of influenza while you were in France. It was 90 degrees Fahrenheit that night. Yet six men in your division were complaining of chills. You remember lying in the trenches with your best friend, Stevie. He was barely awake. His face and lips were blue. You left to fix some scaffolding, but when you came back, he was dead.

Turn the page.

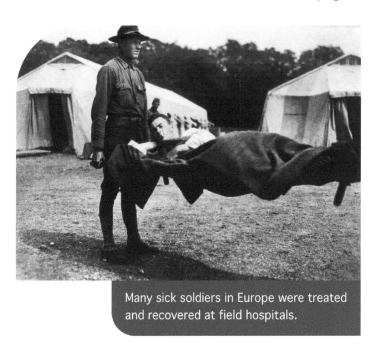

Many sick soldiers in Europe were treated and recovered at field hospitals.

"So what do you think?" your father asks.

"Huh? What?" you ask, shaking your head. You were deep in thought and hadn't been listening.

"I said, how about you come to work with me tomorrow? Maybe the boss can find something for you," he says.

You hesitate. "I'm not sure any of us should be going anywhere," you say.

To insist that your family quarantine themselves, turn to page 21.

To go to your father's work the next day, turn to page 24.

If your brother-in-law is sick, you don't want to be around anyone who was exposed to him. In your time in France, you've seen influenza up close. This flu is different than what has come before. It needs to be taken seriously.

But avoiding the flu isn't your main reason for going out tonight. You haven't seen your fiancée since you left for the war. She doesn't even know you're home yet. As you sneak out the front door of the apartment, all you can think about is how surprised Mandi will be to see you.

Ten minutes later, you arrive outside her family's home. You use the door knocker and stand on the front stoop nervously. In your hand is a bouquet of fresh flowers from the corner store.

As luck would have it, Mandi is the one to open the door. She lets out a high-pitched squeal and wraps her arms around you. In her hurry, she crushes the flowers in your hands.

Turn the page.

"Uh, these are for you," you say, handing her the smooshed flowers.

"They're beautiful," she laughs.

"Well, they *were*," you say, grinning.

She sets the flowers down on a table right inside the front door.

"Well, what are we waiting for?" you say. "Want to go out and hit the town?"

Mandi grabs her coat. "You're kidding, right? Where to first?" she asks.

To head to a movie, turn to page 26.
To go for a walk, turn to page 28.

"You all need to take this flu seriously!" you blurt out.

The room is quiet for a second. Then your mother breaks the silence. "Don't start this with us," she says. "We've already heard it all from Linda next door. What are we going to do, hide away forever? Linda still wears a mask when she leaves the apartment! Can you believe it? The flu came and went, like it always does."

THUMP!

The loud noise takes you off guard. You look over at your sister, who's now laying on the floor.

"Caroline!" shouts your mother.

You pick up your sister and gently lay her on the couch. Her lips look a familiar shade of blue. Suddenly, she wakes up.

"Are you okay?" you ask.

Turn the page.

Caroline doesn't answer. She begins coughing fiercely. Your mother hands her a handkerchief. She makes eye contact with you as she leans over her daughter.

TREASURY DEPARTMENT
UNITED STATES PUBLIC HEALTH SERVICE

INFLUENZA

Spread by Droplets sprayed from Nose and Throat

Cover each COUGH and SNEEZE with handkerchief.

Spread by contact.

AVOID CROWDS.

If possible, WALK TO WORK.

Do not spit on floor or sidewalk.

Do not use common drinking cups and common towels.

Avoid excessive fatigue.

If taken ill, go to bed and send for a doctor.

The above applies also to colds, bronchitis, pneumonia, and tuberculosis.

People were encouraged to follow several rules, such as wearing a mask and avoiding large crowds, to avoid spreading the flu.

"Okay, fine," says your mother. "So, what do we do?"

For the next two weeks, your family stays home and quarantines. Although there are a few scary nights, your sister never has to go to a hospital. The rest of the family only develops minor symptoms. For some reason, you never show any signs of the flu. But then, you never did in France either.

After the weeks pass, your mother catches you as you head to the front door.

"Where are you off to?" she asks.

"I owe Mandi a fancy dinner," you say.

"Well, be sure to wear your mask," says your mother.

THE END

To follow another path, turn to page 9.
To learn more about the Influenza Pandemic of 1918, turn to page 101.

"It's seven cents now?" you say as your father pays the fare at the train station.

"Prices went up while you were gone," he says. "The trains have been less crowded lately. There are a lot of people still scared of the flu."

You shrug and follow your dad onto the waiting train. The car is full. It makes you wonder what it was like before the flu hit.

An older man holding a handkerchief to his face stands next to you. A few other passengers are wearing homemade masks. One woman wears something that looks like a simple cloth napkin. It has two ear holes cut into the fabric.

Your father coughs.

"Shouldn't we be wearing masks?" you ask.

"I've told you," he says. "The worst has passed. What? You think we're going to wear those things forever?"

Twenty minutes later, you arrive at the furniture factory where your father works. There's a sign posted on the door. It reads: PLANT CLOSED UNTIL FURTHER NOTICE.

"What's this?" your father says. "Why would they close?"

You try to answer, but he can't hear you over the sound of his own coughing.

"Let's head home, pop," you say.

You both go home, but your father never returns to work. In less than a week, he dies of pneumonia caused by the flu. You're the man of the house now. It's up to you to take care of your family.

THE END

To follow another path, turn to page 9.
To learn more about the Influenza Pandemic of 1918, turn to page 101.

"The films the Army showed us weren't really up to snuff," you say, as Mandi takes your arm. "Anything good at the movies around here?"

"I think there's a recent Charlie Chaplin movie playing down the street," says Mandi. "But they've been showing a lot of repeats lately. I heard Hollywood shut down production for a while."

"Yeah?" you say. You start to walk toward the movie house. It's only a few blocks away.

"They closed all the theaters around here back in September," says Mandi. "They were saying in the papers that so many people crammed into the theater was helping to spread the flu."

When you arrive at the movie house, you pay ten cents for a pair of tickets and head inside. The theater isn't too crowded. It's a relief. You just got back from some very crowded conditions in France. You're thankful for the space.

There's a cartoon showing on the screen. A little boy and his dog are washing dishes.

"It doesn't look like they're doing it now," whispers Mandi, "but they were spacing people out before. They skipped whole rows so people didn't cough on each other."

You hear a man coughing behind you.

"That would be nice," you say quietly.

After a newsreel and the short movie, you and Mandi are ready to leave. Thanks to the man's constant cough, you're happy to leave anyway.

To call it a night and go home, turn to page 38.
To head out for a bite to eat, turn to page 40.

"With the sickness that's going around," you say, "how about we just go for a walk?"

It's a nice night, so Mandi doesn't mind. With her arm in yours, you head down the street toward Boston Common. It's Boston's biggest park, and one of your favorite spots in the city. You've missed it.

You walk down Tremont Street with the park in view. As you get closer, you begin to hear a strange chant. Then you notice the crowd. Some people are carrying signs. One bright sign reads FREEDOM AND LIBERTY in big letters. Finally, you make out what they're chanting.

"Breathe free! No masks! Breathe free! No masks!"

Neither you nor Mandi are wearing masks at the moment. You're outside, and you don't feel sick. You didn't even think about it.

"They have these rallies all the time," says Mandi. "Things used to be stricter, but the mayor has relaxed most everything now. I don't know what they're still complaining about."

"Mandi!" a voice calls from across the street. You turn just as a young woman about your age rushes up to you. "So you *are* coming!" she says.

"To what?" you ask.

"I completely forgot," says Mandi. "I was supposed to go to a party tonight," she says.

"Right around the corner," says the woman. "And if you're the young man Mandi's told us about, you should come, too!"

To see what the anti-mask rally is all about, turn to page 30.

To go to the party, turn to page 32.

"I'm not really up for a party," you say to Mandi. "Honestly, I'm pretty tired from all the travelling."

"Okay. Hopefully I'll get a chance to meet you properly later," the woman says with a wink. "Don't want to be late for the party!"

She gives Mandi a quick hug and leaves. Then you and Mandi head further into the park.

"They call these guys 'mask slackers,'" Mandi says, nodding her head toward the rally.

"Really?"

"The papers say we don't need masks much anymore. But others say a second flu wave is coming," says Mandi. "It's hard to know what to believe."

"You can't trust the papers!" a man suddenly shouts at you both. Spit flies from his mouth as he screams. He seems almost hysterical. "Masks only help the mask-makers!"

You and Mandi hurry away from the man. He continues to shout at you, even as you rush down the street. "This is the land of the free! Let us breathe!"

With the night all but ruined, you decide to head home.

The next morning, you're not feeling too well. Two days later, things get much worse. Your body aches all over. You're constantly coughing. And your lips have taken on a blue color.

By the following Tuesday, you stop breathing. Mandi brings roses to your funeral from your favorite corner store.

THE END

To follow another path, turn to page 9.
To learn more about the Influenza Pandemic of 1918, turn to page 101.

"My name's Helen," the woman tells you, as you approach an apartment building.

"Where are my manners?" Mandi says. "Sorry, Helen. I should've introduced you."

You follow Helen and Mandi through an unlocked door and up a flight of stairs. You're not quite sure you're in the party mood. But you don't want your night with Mandi to end either.

When you reach the fifth floor, you ask, "Just how high up is this party?"

Helen laughs. "We're almost there," she says. You reach the top of the staircase, and Helen pushes open a door.

You hear a rush of voices and feel a gust of cold air. The party is on the roof.

It's a relief to be out in the open. The thought of spending time in a crowded, stuffy room seems like a silly mistake to make right now.

"Mandi!" a man says, stepping forward and giving Mandi a hug. She gives him a polite fake kiss on the cheek.

"And you must be her fella," says the man. He offers you his hand, and you shake it. Then he pulls it back abruptly. He coughs hard into his closed fist.

Turn the page.

People were reminded to cover their coughs to prevent the spread of flu and other diseases.

PREVENT DISEASE

CARELESS
SPITTING, COUGHING, SNEEZING,
SPREAD INFLUENZA
and TUBERCULOSIS

RENSSELAER COUNTY TUBERCULOSIS ASSOCIATION, TROY, N.Y.

"Heard a lot about you," he says after he recovers.

"This is David," says Mandi. "Helen's boyfriend."

You look around for Helen. She seems to have disappeared. Then you hear a scream from across the roof.

Panic builds up in your chest. But then you realize that Helen is just overreacting. A raindrop hits you square on the forehead. And then another.

"As if the cold wasn't bad enough!" says Helen.

"Okay, all," says David. "Let's move this party inside. Apartment 4B."

As the party-goers begin to shuffle toward the stairwell, you look at Mandi.

"What do you think?" she asks.

To head inside, go to page 35.
To call it a night and go home, turn to page 37.

You and Mandi follow David downstairs to his apartment. It's a fairly big place. But the apartment is still packed. You can't take a step without bumping into one stranger or another.

"Kinda makes me want to wear a mask again," says Mandi.

"So, you're back from the frontlines," interrupts David. "See any action?"

"Oh," you say. "Yeah. Yes, I did."

"Well, give us a story, old boy!" says David. He coughs again. He's smiling, but you're not in the mood to think about the Great War. You came here to relax. You don't feel like thinking about the worst days of your life.

"Another time," you say. "Excuse me."

You work your way back to Mandi. You stay at the party for a couple more hours. But you don't really enjoy yourself.

Turn the page.

Your mind drifts to the war. You think about some of the friends you'll never see again. You think about your best friend, Stevie, who caught the flu and was dead within the same day.

A few days later, you're thinking of Stevie even more. You struggle to breathe on your bed. Your chest aches as you cough more than you've ever coughed in your life.

The day before you die, your mother tells you that Mandi has caught the flu as well. You think of Stevie. Then you wonder if you'll see him again when it's all over.

THE END

To follow another path, turn to page 9.
To learn more about the Influenza Pandemic of 1918, turn to page 101.

You take a look inside the crowded apartment 4B. That's enough for you. "I think we ought to head home," you say to Mandi.

The two of you walk down the stairs and into the street. It's sprinkling outside, but neither of you seem to care.

The following week, you bump into Helen on the street. She's wearing a gauze mask over her nose and mouth. You hardly recognize her.

"You look well," says Helen. "You're probably the only person from the party who is! Everyone's caught the flu. David worst of all."

You take a few steps back, and then excuse yourself. You walk back home, happy to be breathing in the clean, brisk November air.

THE END

To follow another path, turn to page 9.
To learn more about the Influenza Pandemic of 1918, turn to page 101.

It's chillier now that you're outside. For the first time since you've been home, it really feels like winter is on the way.

"I think we should call it a night," you say to Mandi.

"Really?" she says. "It's so early and you just got home!"

"I know. But I'm not sure it's a good idea to be out and about right now."

Mandi sighs but takes your arm. "I'm so sick of being cooped up," she says.

You walk her to her front door, and she gives you a goodnight kiss.

"Let's make plans for next week," you say. She smiles and heads inside. You can't be sure, but you think you hear her sneeze behind the door.

A few days later, you stop by Mandi's house. This time, her mother answers the door.

"Hi, Mrs. H.," you say.

"It's so good to see you," her mother says. That comes as a surprise. You don't think Mandi's mother has ever been happy to see you.

"You, too," you say. "Is Mandi home?"

"I'm afraid Mandi's taken ill," she says. "She's been doing nothing but coughing and sneezing for the last few days."

You head home, feeling full of worry for your fiancée. Luckily, in a week's time, Mandi has fully recovered from the flu. Regardless, you decide your next date should be somewhere outside.

THE END

To follow another path, turn to page 9.
To learn more about the Influenza Pandemic of 1918, turn to page 101.

You're greeted by the smell of greasy burgers and fries as you and Mandi enter the local diner.

"Sit anywhere you'd like," says the man behind the counter. You look around the small restaurant. Most of the booths are full. Two or three people have masks covering their noses and mouths. It's a strange sight.

"This looks good," says Mandi, pointing to the booth near the window. You nod and sit down across from her. Just then, the woman in the booth behind you blows her nose.

A waitress who looks no older than sixteen steps up to your table. She wipes her nose on her apron and says, "What can I get you?"

*   *   *

The cheeseburgers were good. But four days later, Mandi gets sick with influenza. You stop by her house, but her mother won't let you in.

Two days later, you get word that both Mandi and her father have died. They had developed pneumonia brought on by the flu.

The war may be over. But the world you've returned to seems just as dangerous.

THE END

To follow another path, turn to page 9.
To learn more about the Influenza Pandemic of 1918, turn to page 101.

The 1918 flu was fast and deadly. A healthy young person could die within days of being infected.

People often wore simple cloth masks to try to prevent spreading the flu.

CHAPTER 3
A SHOP IN ASHEVILLE

You step off the streetcar at the train station as the chill of the wind hits you. It is October in 1918. It's so cold that when you see a man with his face covered in gauze, you mistake it for a scarf. Then you see a woman wearing what looks like a washcloth on her face. It's a simple brown piece of fabric with two holes on each end. The holes are looped around her ears.

"Oh, I see," you say softly to yourself. You've read about these face masks in the newspaper. You're just not used to seeing them in person. As you walk to the entrance of the train station, you pass four more people wearing similar masks. It's strange to see an Asheville city block resemble a hospital ward.

Turn the page.

You don't have to wait long for the train from Wilmington. After the train slows to a halt, you see your wife shuffling through a sea of people. She holds a handkerchief up to her face.

"Emily!" you say. She gives you a hug.

"Where's your mask, sweetheart?" she asks.

"I do feel a bit out of place without one," you say. "Today is the first time I've really seen them being used."

"Everyone is wearing them in Wilmington," Emily says through the muffle of her handkerchief. "The Spanish Flu has gotten just awful there."

You walk back toward the trolley stop. On the way, Emily tells you about her visit with her sister.

"It was awful," she says, "You wouldn't believe it. Caskets are stacked up six or seven high at the train station!"

"Really?" you ask.

"You find out someone is sick one day. Then the next day they're just . . . gone."

Soon, the trolley lets you off at Pack Square. You and Emily walk a block to your corner store, and she waits as you unlock the front door. There's a jingle of the bell above your head as you enter. You turn the sign from "Closed" to "Open." Then you follow Emily behind the counter.

"Have you thought about shutting the place down?" she asks.

"The store?" you ask. "Why would we want to do that?"

"Because of the flu," says Emily. "I was reading in *The Asheville Citizen* that they've already closed up churches and schools. I think that's the best way to keep everyone safe."

Turn the page.

"We can't shut down the store, Em," you say. "Money is tight. And it's not too bad here. Mrs. Richards down the street got sick. Her son might have it, too. But it doesn't seem much worse than the usual flu."

"Oh no, I've seen it firsthand," says Emily. "It's definitely worse."

"They said there's less than a hundred cases here," you reply

"So far," says Emily. "Just you wait."

Asheville is a mountain town. People like to come here for a break from the Southern heat or for the fresh mountain air. With the many clinics that treat tuberculosis, the sick have always been among the visitors.

"I think we should go to Mother's cabin for a month or so," says Emily. "We should have enough in the bank to tide us over."

In the early 1900s, people in small towns often relied on small local shops for much of their food and goods.

"But we have customers to think of," you say.

"They can walk a few more blocks for their taffy and newspapers," she says in a sarcastic voice. Your store sells much more than that, but you don't feel like arguing any further.

To keep the store open, turn to page 48.

To close the shop and head to the country, turn to page 50.

You didn't see what Emily saw in Wilmington. But you think she might be exaggerating a little. You decide to keep your shop open for now.

Emily isn't happy with your choice. When you go to work the next day, she stays in your apartment above the store. You miss her company. But you and your employee, Thomas, can handle the customers.

Thomas is in his mid-twenties. He's one of the best salesmen you've ever seen. He can convince someone to buy not just a can of soup, but a newspaper, a candy, and a cup of coffee too. Thomas just seems to have a way with people.

So it's strange when Thomas enters the shop without a smile on his face.

"Are you doing okay, Tommy?" you ask.

"Just a little tired," says Thomas. Then he flashes his smile. "I'll be fine with a cup of coffee."

As Thomas heads behind the counter, you hear the ringing of the bell above the door. An older man walks in and takes a look around the store. You think he says something, but it's hard to hear him with his mask on.

"Can I help you?" you ask. He grunts and then leaves.

"That was odd," you say.

"Was it?" says Emily from behind you. She was watching the whole time. Handing you a homemade cloth mask, she says, "If you're going to keep the shop open, you at least need to be safe about it."

To wear the cloth mask, turn to page 53.

To continue with business as usual, turn to page 55.

You frown as you lock the front door of the shop. With suitcases in hand, you and Emily are soon in your Model T car driving to the mountains beyond North Asheville.

When your mother-in-law died a few years ago, she left Emily a small cabin in the woods. You aren't a big fan of the country. But the property isn't far. You and Emily go there for a weekend once in a while or on a holiday.

It takes about an hour to get there. A few times you think the car won't make it up the winding mountain roads. You bought it used, after all. But it keeps chugging along.

You turn off the road onto the dusty lane that leads over a tiny brook. The cabin sits on a grassy meadow on a mountaintop. The views are spectacular, even from the car. But while the Blue Ridge Mountains are impressive, you like that you can see all of downtown Asheville far below.

Leaves crunch under your feet as you carry your belongings into the cabin. You've brought plenty of fresh food from the store. Plus, the cabin is well-stocked with a variety of canned food, bags of flour, and other necessities.

You walk inside. The warm sunlit air from the windows is unexpected. You may not need as much firewood as you thought for the wood stove.

Turn the page.

The cabin has only four rooms—a tiny bedroom, a little kitchen, a bathroom, and a nice living room. Although modest, the place is larger than your apartment downtown. You worry about the store, but you spend the next month enjoying the cabin as best you can.

One day, there's a knock at the door. Emily opens it and greets an old woman you recognize. It's Mrs. Baxter from the farm down the mountain.

"I'm so glad to see a friendly face," says Mrs. Baxter. "We need help. Nathan, my youngest, he's very sick."

Emily looks away from Mrs. Baxter and across the room to you.

To help Mrs. Baxter, turn to page 57.
To refuse to help her, turn to page 58.

You sigh and take the mask from Emily's hands. You're not sure how she made it so quickly. It's made of white gauze with two strings on each side to tie behind your head. You tie it on, but you feel a little silly.

Emily passes the other mask to Thomas. You nod at him. He puts his mask on as well. "Thank you, ma'am," he says.

"Think nothing of it, Thomas," she answers. Emily turns and heads to the back room. You're sure she's going back up to the apartment. She's still mad at you, after all.

The bell for the front door jingles and you get back to work.

Weeks pass. Business is slow. Emily was right about the flu. Every day you hear about more and more people getting sick. The news from other cities is even worse.

Turn the page.

"Here you go, honey," Emily says as she sets down a box on the counter. "Just in."

You open the lid to see twelve small jars of Bromo Quinine. It's a laxative made by E. W. Grove. The package promises that it will cure influenza before it even starts. You have your doubts. But at this point, you're willing to try anything.

"You got any cigars?" a voice asks from the door.

"Excuse me, sir," says Emily. "Face masks are required for entry."

The man ignores her as he steps inside the store. He wipes his runny nose on his sleeve and begins to look around.

To throw the customer out, turn to page 60.
To ignore him and let him shop, turn to page 66.

You thank Emily for the mask. You put it in your apron and never think of it again.

The week passes as usual. But when Friday arrives, there's no sign of Thomas. On your lunch break, you ask Emily to mind the counter. Then you head to Thomas's apartment to check on him.

Thomas only lives a few blocks from the store. A brisk walk in the fresh air might do you a little good. You tip your hat to some familiar faces as you walk by. Nearly everyone is wearing a mask. You shake your head. They're all so afraid of this Spanish Flu. They're missing out on the simple joys of life.

You arrive at Thomas's building. Suddenly, the door opens.

"May I help you?" a woman asks as she leaves the building.

Turn the page.

"Just checking up on my employee," you say. "Thomas is scheduled to work today."

"Thomas O'Neil?" asks the woman. "Oh, he's caught the flu. I saw him just yesterday. He looked absolutely terrible."

The woman exits and heads down the street. You decide to leave Thomas alone. Perhaps he's sleeping. If he's sick, he needs his rest. But you've been working closely with him. What should you do?

To go back to work as usual, turn to page 68. To close the shop and quarantine, turn to page 70.

Mrs. Baxter had ridden up to your cabin in an old-fashioned horse and buggy. While many people in Asheville have automobiles, she never wanted such a luxury.

You follow her to her farmhouse and into her son's bedroom. There, Nathan lies on his bed. He coughs heavily, and his face has a blueish tint to it. You've never seen anything like it before.

"I think he needs the hospital," you say.

"I don't want to move him," says Mrs. Baxter. "He's much too sick for that. I was hoping you had some tonics. Emily told me about your store. Surely you have some sort of medicines that could help."

To take Nathan to the hospital, turn to page 62.

To give him some of the medicine you brought, turn to page 64.

"I'm sorry," you say. You walk across the room to the door. "I'm not a doctor. I don't think I can be of any help."

"Yes, but my Nathan—" Mrs. Baxter says.

"Sorry, again," you say abruptly. "I hope he gets better soon." You shut the front door.

"We should help her," Emily says.

"There's nothing we can do," you say. "We came up here to get away from the flu."

"Well, it doesn't sit well with me," says Emily.

She walks away and sits by the stove. "At least make a fire!" she says. She seems more than a little upset.

You don't see Mrs. Baxter again for another month. You're driving down to the city for more supplies. As you pass Mrs. Baxter's farm, you see her out for a morning walk.

"How's Nathan?" you ask.

"He passed three weeks ago," she says matter-of-factly. Then she turns and walks swiftly away from your car.

As you head to Asheville, you feel guilt creep over you. If you had helped, you and Emily might be sick or dying right now. But you would have at least done all you could. The guilt you feel now will haunt you more than any other memory of this horrible pandemic.

THE END

To follow another path, turn to page 9.
To learn more about the Influenza Pandemic of 1918, turn to page 101.

"If you don't have a mask, I'm going to have to ask you to leave," you say.

"Ask all you want. Don't mean I'm gonna listen to you." The man sneezes and doesn't bother to cover his mouth. "What kinda cigars you got?" he asks again.

You step out from behind the counter and move closer to the customer. He's older than you. But he's taller than you as well. This whole situation has you feeling pretty nervous.

"Please leave, sir," you say, raising your voice.

"I'll do what I please," he says. A bit of spit flies from his mouth.

You grab the man's arm and lead him to the door. You're surprised when he doesn't fight you.

"Out!" you say. The man steps away from you. Then he spits on the ground.

"If you don't want my business, fine!" he shouts. He begins to stumble away. "My money works just as good at the next store!"

You head back inside. Emily smiles at you. You shrug.

Months pass. You make it through the pandemic with your health intact. It looks like Emily was right all along. It paid to take extra care. Not that you would ever admit that to her.

THE END

To follow another path, turn to page 9.
To learn more about the Influenza Pandemic of 1918, turn to page 101.

It takes a half an hour, but you finally convince Mrs. Baxter to let Nathan go to the hospital. You help carry him out to your Model T.

You look over at Nathan from time to time as you drive down the mountain. He's probably twenty years old at most. He might be even younger. It seems odd that the flu has taken such a hold of him. In past flu seasons, it's always the elderly that suffer the most.

You adjust the mask on your face and lean against your car door and its open window.

You told Mrs. Baxter you were headed to the hospital. But you know that it's pointless. The newspaper has been reporting that the hospital is full for some time. However, the next best thing has opened on Woodfin Street. The American Red Cross has converted a high school into an emergency ward. So, that's where you take Nathan.

The Red Cross set up emergency clinics and prepared to help flu patients in several U.S. cities.

The nurse at the front door says they have a few spare beds. You leave Nathan in her care, then drive back up the mountain.

Unfortunately, it was too late. The Red Cross could do nothing for Nathan. You find out weeks later that he has died. You did what you could, but sometimes even that's not enough.

THE END

To follow another path, turn to page 9.
To learn more about the Influenza Pandemic of 1918, turn to page 101.

You argue with Mrs. Baxter for more than an hour. It's no use. She doesn't want Nathan going to the hospital.

"Do you have anything to make him more comfortable?" she asks.

"I'll see what I can do," you say.

You drive back up the mountain and look through your cabinets.

"I've heard putting sulfur in his shoes can help," says Emily.

"What?"

"It was in the paper. A man working at the graveyard uses a bit of sulfur sprinkled in his shoes. He's never gotten sick a day in his life," she says.

You don't have any sulfur. Even if you did, you doubt it would do anything to help.

However, none of the other remedies seem much better. You fill a bag with some laxative pills, a bottle of mouthwash, and even a bit of whiskey. You've heard rumors that all these things could help.

An hour later, you drop off the supplies. You help Mrs. Baxter change Nathan's sheets and tidy up his room. You tell Mrs. Baxter that you'll check in on her again in a day's time.

But the next morning, your throat hurts just to swallow. You begin to have terrible coughing fits. A few days later, Emily holds your hand as you pass away. Before you die, you notice that Emily's own cough has gotten worse.

THE END

To follow another path, turn to page 9.
To learn more about the Influenza Pandemic of 1918, turn to page 101.

You turn your back from the man and let him shop. Emily storms off into the back room in a huff. If this man doesn't want to wear a mask, that's his business. Your business is the store. You can't afford to lose any customers with the way things are going.

"Can I help you find something?" you ask.

"These cigars seem pretty cheap," the man says, looking over the counter at your tobacco section. The man begins to cough. He doesn't cover his mouth. After his fit is over, he wipes his runny eyes. Then he sneezes hard just as Thomas walks by.

"What kind of operation you runnin' here?" says the man. "Ain't nothing of quality in the whole place." He stumbles as he turns and pushes his way out the door.

Thomas wipes his face with a handkerchief and adjusts his face mask. "Want me to put out those Bromo tablets?" he asks.

Treat COLDS in the First Stage!

Colds Go Thru 3 Stages and They're Far Easier Stopped in the First than in the Second or Third!

IT PAYS to know something about colds. They're a great cause of prolonged sickness and financial loss.

A cold ordinarily progresses through three stages. The first is the Dry stage, the first 24 hours. The second is the Watery stage, from 1 to 3 days. The third is the Mucous Secretion stage.

The first stage is the time to "nail" a cold. It is twice as easily relieved then as in the second or third stages. In fact, to let a cold run beyond the first stage is taking chances. For a cold can quickly develop into something serious.

The Wise Measure

The wise thing to do when you catch cold is to take Grove's Laxative Bromo Quinine. This famous tablet stops a cold quickly because it does the four things necessary.

First, it opens the bowels, gently but thoroughly, the first step in expelling a cold.

Second, it combats the cold germs in the system and reduces the fever.

Third, it relieves the headache and that grippy feeling.

Fourth, it tones the entire system and helps fortify against further attack.

This is the treatment a cold requires and anything less is inviting trouble.

Grove's Laxative Bromo Quinine is utterly harmless and may be taken with perfect safety. The fact that it has been the leading cold and grippe tablet of the world for years attests to its safety as well as efficiency.

Now — 20% More for Your Money! Every drug store in America sells Grove's Laxative Bromo Quinine in two sizes—30c and 50c. In the interest of economy, buy the 50c size. It gives you 20% more for your money. Always ask for Grove's Laxative Bromo Quinine by the full name and look for the letters L B Q stamped on each tablet. Look for an ulterior motive when a substitute is offered.

> A Cold is an Internal Infection and Requires Internal Treatment

GROVE'S LAXATIVE
BROMO QUININE

"Better take one for yourself," you say, nodding.

But all the medicine in the world won't help Thomas now. Within the week, he is sick with the flu. You learn later that twenty- to forty-year-old people are the group hardest hit by this disease.

Thomas dies a few days later. You don't risk going to the funeral. It wouldn't have mattered, though. You get sick the next day.

THE END

To follow another path, turn to page 9.
To learn more about the Influenza Pandemic of 1918, turn to page 101.

There's nothing you can do for Thomas. But you can keep the store going. That way, when Thomas gets better, he'll have a job waiting for him. It wouldn't do either of you any good to take away your source of income.

On the way back to the store, you feel some pain in your back.

"I shouldn't have tried to lift those heavy boxes this morning," you say to yourself. But with Thomas gone, you didn't have much choice. The store needs to stay stocked.

"You look terrible," says Emily a few hours later.

"I just hurt my back is all," you say.

But that's not the whole truth. Sure, your back hurts. But now your arms ache too. Your legs feel weak. Your nose is dripping constantly. When the work day finally ends, you head upstairs to sleep.

You never leave your bed. You've got the flu, and it soon worsens to pneumonia. You have trouble breathing, and you can't stop coughing.

Forty-eight hours later, you take your last gasp of air.

Emily closes the shop to attend your funeral. She never reopens the store again.

THE END

To follow another path, turn to page 9.
To learn more about the Influenza Pandemic of 1918, turn to page 101.

You head back to the store, grab a broom, and start sweeping. When Emily walks in from the storeroom, she has a surprised look on her face.

"What are you up to?" she asks.

"I decided to close up for the day," you say.

"And why is that?"

"Tommy is home sick with influenza," you say. "I think you and I should keep to ourselves for the next week."

"I'll get started on dinner," Emily says through an understanding smile. "Sounds like my famous chicken soup is in order."

For the next week, you and Emily stay quarantined in your apartment above the store. You watch as customers walk up to the shop's door, then walk away when they find it closed. You're losing money, but there's nothing you can do.

By the end of the week, you start to show signs of the flu yourself. Luckily, it's a mild case. Another week passes and you feel like your old self.

You head downstairs and turn the "Closed" sign around to "Open." You look around the shop. You doubt it will ever feel the same. You just learned that Thomas has died. You can't help but feel at least partially to blame.

THE END

To follow another path, turn to page 9.
To learn more about the Influenza Pandemic of 1918, turn to page 101.

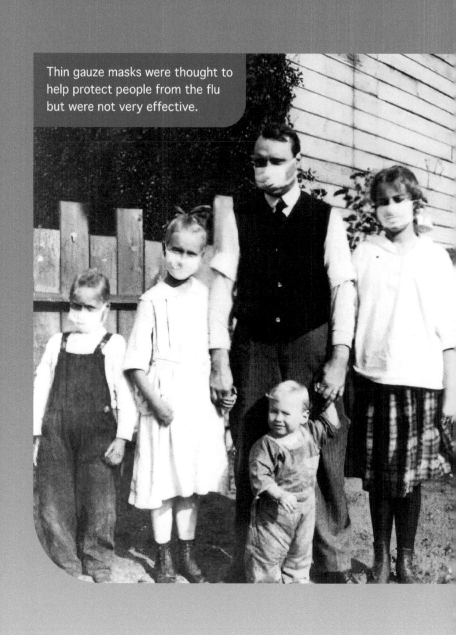

Thin gauze masks were thought to help protect people from the flu but were not very effective.

CHAPTER 4
NEW YORK NIGHTMARE

As you walk to your school in Brooklyn, New York, you can't believe how nice the weather is. It's early October, but you feel a bit warm in your light jacket. You usually love the fall. But this year is different.

Influenza has arrived in the Big Apple. Everyone on the streets seems to be in more of a hurry. Many are wearing face masks made out of gauze or fabric.

You're not sure how much the flimsy gauze helps. But you're wearing your mask anyway. You look down at your son, Henry. The second grader isn't wearing a mask. But you aren't too concerned. Few children wear them in your neighborhood.

Turn the page.

A man tips his hat as he passes you. You don't see much of his face beneath his large mask. You're glad he's being responsible. Because where you're headed, people aren't quite as sensible.

You're a second-grade teacher in New York City. There are nearly one million children in the public school system. Unlike adults, most children have little concern for personal cleanliness. To them, dirt and muck are just part of an average day.

Even worse, the children in your class don't think twice about a friend's sneeze. Most have trouble remembering to cover their own mouths when they cough. Henry is definitely among that number.

You're fighting an uphill battle. But keeping children safe is part of your job. This is what you signed up for, even if you've never seen anything as serious as this so-called Spanish Flu.

As you arrive at school, you see your good friend Peggy is waiting for you.

"Hello," she says. Peggy's daughter is in your class. "Do you have a minute?" Peggy asks.

"Run along," you say to Henry. He's more than a little happy to run and join his friends inside. He's already through the front door of the building before you say another word.

"What do you need?" you ask Peggy.

"I wanted you to know that I'm pulling Amelia out of school after today," Peggy says.

"Oh," you say, surprised. "Why is that?"

"I just don't think it's safe here with the flu and all," she says.

"Well, we take plenty of precautions—"

Turn the page.

"I know," she interrupts. "But to be honest, there aren't many schools still open in the state. New York must think it's special or something. Outside of the city, everyone is closing."

You think about this for a moment. "Thanks for telling me," you say.

As Peggy walks away, you wonder if you're doing the right thing. Are you and Henry really safe in a crowded school?

To continue your day as normal, go to page 77.
To take Henry home, turn to page 80.

You're all but certain that Peggy is wrong. After all, you know the majority of the children in public school live in tenements. Their tiny apartments have little to no fresh air. But your school's rooms are large and airy, and you keep your windows open to help move that air around.

Peggy is free to make her own decisions about her family's safety. But so are you. And you and Henry are staying put. You walk up the stairs, straighten your dress, and enter your classroom. The students are talking to each other. They seem louder than normal today.

"Settle down, class," you say. Most of the children listen. Henry's friend, James, does not.

"I had a little bird, and its name was Enza. I opened the window, and in flew Enza!" James sings. You've heard the little rhyme before. The kids sing it while skipping rope after school.

Turn the page.

"That's enough, James," you say in a strict voice. He giggles a little. But he stops singing.

You walk over to the row of windows in your classroom. You begin to open each one. "That's a funny little song," you say to the class. "But did you know that we don't have to worry about influenza coming in through the window? Fresh air is actually a good way to fight the flu."

The children don't seem impressed. But you know a good way to keep the flu from spreading is by circulating the air. You learned this from a tuberculosis scare when you first started teaching.

"Now, let's all line up," you say. Your comment is met with plenty of groans from the class. They move slowly, standing up in front of their desks. They're tired of this daily routine. You've been doing it for weeks now. It's part of the school's safety program.

Every morning you have to check each child for red eyes or runny noses. You need to make sure no one is sneezing or coughing. So far, only one student has shown any symptoms. That's probably why the kids all seem annoyed with you.

You need to make sure everyone is safe, but maybe this daily checkup is being overprotective. Maybe the kids need a break today.

To stick with the school policy, turn to page 81.

To skip the morning wellness check, turn to page 83.

Several schools started holding classes outdoors to avoid spreading the flu.

You decide to play it extra safe. After school, you inform the principal that you'll be leaving your job. Henry will be taking a break from school as well.

When you arrive home, you begin to doubt your decision. Your husband died a few years ago from tuberculosis. Your teacher's salary is your only income. You and Henry have only enough money for the rest of the month. You need to act fast, but what will you do?

To look for another job, turn to page 87.

To stay home with Henry, turn to page 89.

You can hear James complaining under his breath. Yet you check each student anyway. Henry is mad, too, but he gets over it soon enough.

From there, the day goes on as normal. Your spelling lesson goes well. Only one child drops his chalkboard on the floor. It's James, of course. Soon enough, it's time for lunch.

The students all march through the hall in a single-file line and head to the courtyard outside. They take their assigned seats at the picnic tables as you pass out their lunches to them.

Suddenly, you hear some noise from inside the school. You walk inside and see an angry man yelling at the principal.

"This is outrageous!" the man shouts. "Mabel was sent home yesterday. My wife and I both work. How are we supposed to watch her all day?"

Turn the page.

You recognize the man. "Mr. Daniels," you say, "I was the one who sent your daughter home. She had a runny nose and a fever, according to the nurse."

"Then you should be the one to let her back in!" he shouts.

For the first time, you notice his daughter Mabel standing in the hallway behind him. Her nose is still runny. You can tell because she hasn't bothered to wipe it.

To let Mabel back in class, turn to page 93.
To refuse to let Mabel come back, turn to page 95.

"I think we can manage one day without a wellness check," you say to your students.

"Hooray!" the children cheer. You let them celebrate for just a moment.

"Okay, children, to your seats," you finally say.

There are plenty of smiles on faces for the rest of the day. The kids seem overjoyed to skip such a minor trouble. It makes sense. Children need to get their own way once in a while. Sometimes, making things slightly easier can make a world of difference.

Things go so well that the next day, you decide to skip the morning check again. Then the next day, too. Pretty soon, it becomes a habit.

The following week, as the children sit at their desks, you hear a sneeze from the back row. To your surprise, you see Henry wiping his nose with his shirt.

Turn the page.

"Henry, are you feeling okay?" you ask.

He tries to answer but sneezes again.

You turn around to face the chalkboard. Your face has turned nearly as pale as the chalk in your hand. Should you take Henry to the nurse as the rules state? You'll certainly get in trouble if you do. But you can't just leave Henry in class where he could get the others sick.

To take Henry to the school nurse, go to page 85.

To ignore his symptoms, turn to page 91.

You summon all of your courage. Then you tell the class to open their books and begin reading silently. You call Henry up to the front.

"We'll be right back," you tell the other students.

You walk Henry out of the room and into the hall. He doesn't say anything. The two of you head toward the nurse's office.

Turn the page.

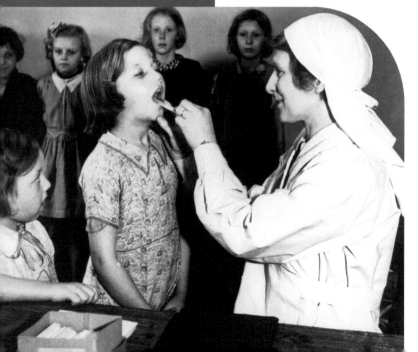

School nurses and teachers regularly checked young students for signs of the flu.

"Come in," says Miss Harrow, when you knock on her door. Miss Harrow is your good friend. As she inspects Henry, you begin talking. You casually mention that you've skipped some morning wellness checks.

"There haven't been any problems. The kids have been in good health, after all," you say.

But the next day, you're called to the principal's office. The principal fires you almost immediately. He says that every day you skipped the wellness check, you put your students at risk.

You and Henry walk home together. You can't believe you lost your job. You don't know how you're going to pay the next month's rent. And Henry's sneezing is getting worse.

THE END

To follow another path, turn to page 9.
To learn more about the Influenza Pandemic of 1918, turn to page 101.

You spend the next week looking for work. The job hunt is harder than you thought. Many businesses are closed due to the flu.

Finally, you find a grocery store that needs someone to mind the counter. You gladly take the position. The hours are long, but the work suits you just fine.

It's Henry you worry about. With no one at home to watch him, Henry spends all of his time with the upstairs neighbors. Their son is in sixth grade. He's home from school as well, and he and Henry play every day. Sometimes they play ball in the empty lot next door. Sometimes they play inside the apartments. You don't always hear what they're up to. Henry is a pretty quiet child.

One day you return home late. You had to organize the entire stockroom at the store. You're tired and ready for bed. Since it's past Henry's bedtime, you tiptoe to his room and peek inside.

Turn the page.

He's sleeping soundly. As you turn around, you hear a cough. But Henry is fast asleep. Then you hear the cough again. It's coming from upstairs. It sounds like the neighbors are coming down with the flu.

You can't afford to miss work. But at the same time, you can't risk the neighbors getting Henry sick. You're not sure what to do.

To go to work as usual, turn to page 97.
To take Henry to work with you, turn to page 98.

You can't bear to leave Henry alone while you go off to work. You decide your best choice is to wait out this epidemic. By November, you're almost out of money. It won't last through December. You and Henry are already living on modest rations.

You hear about a soup kitchen down the street. You spend more than a few nights there. One night, a man across from you coughs through the entire meal. A few days later, you begin to feel tired. Your nose runs and your eyes start to water.

Turn the page.

Many hungry people relied on soup kitchens for a hot meal during the flu pandemic.

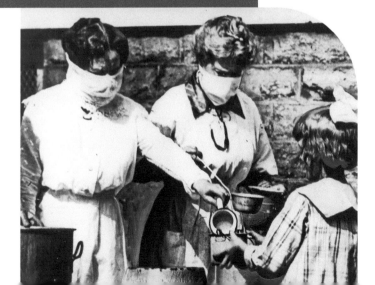

The next morning, you let Henry play outside. You say goodbye, and he runs out the door. He's excited to see his friends' faces.

When the door closes behind Henry, you fall asleep. You have no idea that you'll never see your son again.

By evening, your body has given up completely. After you die, Henry is sent to Massachusetts to live with your cousins.

Like many affected by the 1918 flu pandemic, Henry is forever changed. He dedicates his life to making sure something like this never happens again. He becomes a doctor of infectious diseases. You would have been so proud of him if you had lived to see him grow up.

THE END

To follow another path, turn to page 9.
To learn more about the Influenza Pandemic of 1918, turn to page 101.

You continue about your day as if nothing is wrong. The other children notice Henry's sneezing and coughing. But you pretend not to.

By the end of the school day, Henry sounds even worse. You realize that you can't hide his symptoms any longer.

You tell the principal that you and Henry won't be at school tomorrow. You need to isolate from the rest of the children in case you both have influenza. The principal agrees. He tells you he'll get someone to take over your class.

When you get back to your small apartment, you're exhausted. You decide to take a nap. But when you wake up, you feel worse.

You soon develop a cough and a runny nose. Your eyes are watery. Your back and body aches. You feel tired, and your throat feels raw from coughing so much. You just can't seem to stop.

Turn the page.

In two days, your coughing finally stops. But so does your breathing. You die from pneumonia as a result of the flu. Henry recovers from the sickness. But like many other orphans, he'll never recover from losing his mother.

THE END

To follow another path, turn to page 9.
To learn more about the Influenza Pandemic of 1918, turn to page 101.

"I think we can make an exception for little Mabel," says the principal.

"Fine," you say. You don't see any point in arguing. "Come with me, Mabel," you say.

"Okay, ma'am," mutters Mabel. Her voice sounds hoarse.

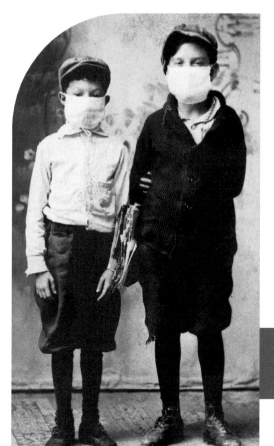

You walk Mabel to class. She sniffs and sneezes as you tell the students to put on their masks.

Turn the page.

Schoolchildren wearing cloth masks in 1918

A week passes. Soon enough, Mabel no longer has a runny nose. In fact, she seems back to her bright, happy self.

But the same isn't true for James. He sat next to Mabel all week. After only one day, he was showing signs of influenza. You had James sent home. It didn't help. In fact, neither you nor Henry ever see him again.

You soon learn that James infected both his mother and his father. They died of pneumonia shortly after coming down with the flu. James lived but was sent to live with his aunt in Ohio.

Every day when you see his empty chair, you wish you would have held your ground. Maybe if you had stood up to the principal, James would still be in your class today.

THE END

To follow another path, turn to page 9.
To learn more about the Influenza Pandemic of 1918, turn to page 101.

"Under no conditions can Mabel come back to school," you say. "Not until she's made a full recovery."

The principal seems surprised by your harsh tone. But he doesn't disagree. He simply turns to Mr. Daniels and waits for his reply.

"Furthermore," you say, "you and your wife should stay at home tending to your daughter. Otherwise, you risk spreading the flu to your coworkers."

Mr. Daniels's face looks beet red. You can tell that he's not happy. "Then Mabel will not be returning to *this* school," he says. "She'll find her education somewhere else."

Mr. Daniels storms away. Mabel stays put. Then suddenly, she realizes that she is supposed to follow her father. She smiles and waves to you. Then she hurries after her angry dad.

Turn the page.

"I'm sorry—" you begin to say to the principal.

"Don't be," the principal says. "He was breaking school policy. You were right. Think no more of it."

You head back outside. You smile as you watch your class eating their lunch.

Mabel never returns to the school. But the rest of your class stays safe. It's a tough year, but you do your best. And in the end, that's all you can do.

THE END

To follow another path, turn to page 9.
To learn more about the Influenza Pandemic of 1918, turn to page 101.

Two more weeks pass. One cold, lonely night when you return home, you call to Henry. But he doesn't answer.

You find him in his room laying on his bed. His skin looks blue. He can barely speak to you. He seems so weak.

You sit up with Henry for the next few days. But soon, you get sick, too. Both you and Henry die of pneumonia soon after.

The New York City school system was one of the safest places to be in 1918. With a nurse on staff at your school, your flu symptoms would have been caught early. Perhaps that would have made all the difference.

THE END

To follow another path, turn to page 9.
To learn more about the Influenza Pandemic of 1918, turn to page 101.

"I'm so bored," Henry complains from the stool in the corner.

"You can always help sweep the back room," you say in a cheery voice.

Henry ignores you. He sighs and goes back to staring at the floor. You feel bad that he's here at work with you. But at least you can keep an eye on him. In the far corner of the small grocery store, a man coughs into his handkerchief.

"There you are!" says a familiar voice, as the door of the shop swings open. You look up to see the principal of your school. Or, you should say, the principal of your *former* school. "Your landlady said you'd taken a job here."

"Hello, sir," you say.

"I need you to come back," says the principal. "We don't have enough staff. I need you back in the classroom."

"I just don't think it's safe," you say. The man in the corner coughs into his handkerchief again. And then again.

You look at the coughing man, then at your old boss. Your decision is easier than you thought.

"Okay," you say. "We'll be back Monday."

While the owner of the grocery store isn't happy, you keep your promise to the principal. You and Henry make it through the pandemic safe and sound. In fact, so does the rest of your class. You sometimes wonder if the same can be said about the customers and staff of the grocery store.

THE END

To follow another path, turn to page 9.
To learn more about the Influenza Pandemic of 1918, turn to page 101.

In September 2021, thousands of white flags were displayed in a park in Washington, D.C., to honor those who died from COVID-19.

In America
Remember

672,689

CHAPTER 5
THE END IN SIGHT

The Influenza Pandemic of 1918 was the greatest global killer the world has ever seen. It is estimated that one in three people were infected by the virus. At least 50 million people died from the flu worldwide. But records at that time were often incomplete. Experts now believe that number is lower than the actual death toll. The 1918 flu may have killed as many as 100 million people.

Compare that to the most recent pandemic—COVID-19. According to the World Health Organization (WHO), more than 1.8 million people died worldwide from COVID-19 in 2020. But the WHO estimates that the true number is closer to 3 million. It's a tragic number, but it pales compared to the 1918 flu.

COVID-19's lower death rate is mostly thanks to modern medicine. Hospitals across the world are better equipped than ever. Doctors and nurses are better educated. Modern technology such as ventilators and vaccines now play a huge role in a patient's survival.

Influenza shook the world from March 1918 until the middle of 1920. The virus would flare up, begin to fade away, then flare up again. The globe suffered three of these terrible waves before this strain of flu disappeared.

Scientists struggle to understand why the 1918 flu went away. Some believe that every person had already been exposed. There were simply no people left to infect. Others believe that the flu continued to mutate until it was no longer harmful to human beings. Whatever happened, the flu left its scars across the world.

However, there was a bit of a silver lining to the flu's dark cloud. The disease sparked a renewed interest in medical science.

The Influenza Pandemic of 1918 caused a shortage of doctors and nurses across the United States. New universities were founded with the purpose of training the next generation of doctors and caregivers. Communities across the country began building more hospitals. Public health officials worked together to better respond to another pandemic.

Many universities offer medical programs for people interested in becoming doctors.

While the strain that caused the 1918 pandemic has long since disappeared, the flu still mutates year after year. A new flu vaccine is issued with each flu season. The Centers for Disease Control and Prevention (CDC) estimates that somewhere between 12,000 to 52,000 people die from influenza-related deaths each year in the United States.

Medical scientists continually research deadly diseases to create new vaccines that can save lives.

That is a high number, but yearly flu shots keep this figure from being much worse. Thanks to modern vaccines, elderly people and those with other health conditions have a much lower risk of dying from the flu.

Science is always learning and moving forward. Theories that people once accepted as true may prove false as more information is gathered. It is an ever-evolving process. But thanks to the hard work of many researchers and health professionals, we haven't seen a crisis as severe as the Influenza Pandemic of 1918. As long as we follow the science, we likely never will again.

TIMELINE OF THE FLU PANDEMIC

JUNE 28, 1914:
WORLD WAR I BEGINS

When Archduke Franz Ferdinand is killed, it sparks a conflict between Austria-Hungary and Germany against Serbia, Russia, Belgium, France, and Great Britain.

APRIL 6, 1917:
UNITED STATES OF AMERICA ENTERS WORLD WAR I

After Germany sinks several U.S. ships, President Woodrow Wilson calls for a declaration of war against Germany.

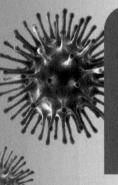

MARCH 4, 1918:
FIRST KNOWN CASE OF THE 1918 FLU EMERGES

The military base at Fort Riley, Kansas, appears to be ground zero for the original 1918 influenza wave.

OCTOBER 1918:
SECOND WAVE OF INFLUENZA HITS THE UNITED STATES' BIGGEST CITIES

After six months of the flu spreading unevenly, major cities including New York City, Philadelphia, Boston, and Chicago suffer major outbreaks. 195,000 people die in the United States in October alone.

NOVEMBER 11, 1918:
WORLD WAR I COMES TO AN END

As the war ends, many cities believe the worst of the flu pandemic has passed. These cities loosen restrictions, but the disease continues to hit communities. The flu is spread in several cases during celebrations of returning soldiers.

JANUARY 1919:
THIRD WAVE OF INFLUENZA STRIKES

A third wave of influenza causes even more death across the globe. Exact numbers are nearly impossible to count, as many deaths went unreported. After a tiring winter and spring, the worst is finally over. By mid-1920, the 1918 flu has disappeared almost completely.

OTHER PATHS TO EXPLORE

>>> The Influenza Pandemic of 1918 played a huge role in World War I. Many believe it forced the fighting to end sooner than expected. What would it have been like to be a French soldier returning home to a small village after being exposed to the flu in the trenches? How would you keep your family safe?

>>> The western United States was more willing to follow mask rules when it came to preventing the flu from spreading. Police in cities like San Francisco would arrest "mask slackers" who refused to wear masks in public. Some experts believe the gauze masks people wore at the time weren't effective in stopping the flu from spreading. Would you have been a supporter of the mask movement? Or would you have been one of the protestors?

>>> Doctors and nurses were hit hard by influenza in 1918. They were forced to work many hours, and many caught the flu while working with infected patients. What would it have been like to be a nurse at a hospital in 1918? How would you react to your coworkers falling ill? Would you continue your mission to help others? Or would you quit your job for yours and your family's safety?

BIBLIOGRAPHY

Barry, John M. *The Great Influenza: The Epic Story of the Deadliest Plague in History*. New York: Penguin Books, 2005.

Brown, Dr. Jeremy. *Influenza: The Hundred-Year Hunt to Cure the Deadliest Disease in History*. New York: Touchstone, 2018.

Cockrell, David L. "'A Blessing in Disguise': The Influenza Pandemic of 1918 and North Carolina's Medical and Public Health Communities," 2016.

Doctor Wise on Influenza. Local Government Board. England, 1919.

Influenza Encyclopedia: The American Influenza Epidemic of 1918–1919. https://www.influenzaarchive.org/cities/city-boston.html#

Lepiarz, Jack. "How Massachusetts Helped Win 'The Great War," WBUR, November 08, 2018, https://www.wbur.org/news/2018/11/08/world-war-i-yankee-division-boston-navy-yard.

Marrin, Albert. *Very, Very, Very Dreadful: The Influenza Pandemic of 1918*. New York: Alfred A. Knopf, 2018.

Pruitt, Sarah. "At Height of the 1918 Pandemic, NYC and Chicago Schools Stayed Open. Here's Why," History.com, August 5, 2020. https://www.history.com/news/spanish-flu-schools-new-york-chicago.

GLOSSARY

commissioner (kuh-MIH-shuh-nuhr)—an official who is in charge of a government department

epidemic (eh-puh-DE-mik)—an infectious disease that spreads quickly through a community or group of people

influenza (in-floo-EN-zuh)—an illness caused by a virus that is like a bad cold with high fever, muscle pain, and weakness

laxative (LAK-suh-tiv)—a medicine that helps relieve constipation

pandemic (pan-DEH-mik)—a disease that spreads over a wide area and infects many people

pneumonia (noo-MOH-nyuh)—a serious disease that infects the lungs and causes them to become filled with thick mucus that makes breathing difficult

quarantine (KWOR-uhn-teen)—to keep a person, animal, or plant away from others to stop a disease from spreading

tenement (TEH-nuh-muhnt)—a rundown apartment building, especially one that is overcrowded and in a poor part of a city

tuberculosis (tuh-buhr-kyoo-LOH-sis)—a disease caused by bacteria in the lungs that causes fever, weight loss, coughing, and difficulty breathing

vaccine (vak-SEEN)—a shot of medicine that helps prevent a disease

READ MORE

Brown, Don. *Fever Year: The Killer Flu of 1918*. Boston: Houghton Mifflin Harcourt, 2019.

Farndon, John. *Plague!: Epidemics and Scourges Through the Ages*. Minneapolis: Hungry Tomato, 2017.

Hubbard, Ben. *Plague: A History of Pestilence and Pandemics*. London: Franklin Watts, 2020.

Messner, Kate. *Plagues and Pandemics*. New York: Random House, 2021.

INTERNET SITES

Britannica: Influenza Pandemic of 1918–19
britannica.com/event/influenza-pandemic-of-1918-1919

CDC: 1918 Pandemic
cdc.gov/flu/pandemic-resources/1918-pandemic-h1n1.html

History: Spanish Flu
history.com/topics/world-war-i/1918-flu-pandemic

ABOUT THE AUTHOR

Author photo courtesy of Dorothy Manning Photography.

Matthew K. Manning is the author of more than 90 books and dozens of comic books. Some of his favorite projects include the popular comic book crossover *Batman/ Teenage Mutant Ninja Turtles Adventures* and the 12-issue series *Marvel Action: Avengers* for IDW, *Exploring Gotham City* for Insight Editions, and the six-volume chapter book series *Xander and the Rainbow-Barfing Unicorns* for Capstone. Manning lives in Asheville, North Carolina with his wife Dorothy and their two daughters, Lillian and Gwendolyn. Visit him online at www.matthewkmanning.com.